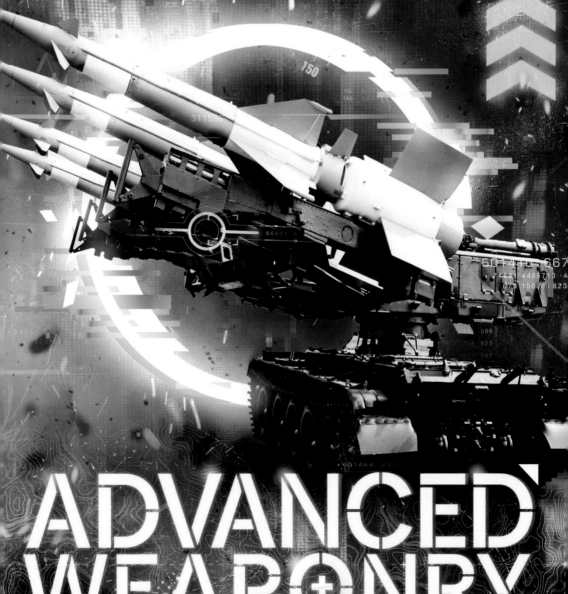

# ADVANCED WEAPONRY

BY MATT CHANDLER

Torque brims with excitement
perfect for thrill-seekers of all kinds.
Discover daring survival skills, explore
uncharted worlds, and marvel at mighty
engines and extreme sports. In *Torque* books,
anything can happen. Are you ready?

This edition first published in 2022 by Bellwether Media, Inc.

No part of this publication may be reproduced in whole or in part without written
permission of the publisher. For information regarding permission, write to
Bellwether Media, Inc., Attention: Permissions Department,
6012 Blue Circle Drive, Minnetonka, MN 55343.

Library of Congress Cataloging-in-Publication Data

LC record for Advanced Weaponry available at: https://lccn.loc.gov/2021051735

Text copyright © 2022 by Bellwether Media, Inc. TORQUE and associated logos are
trademarks and/or registered trademarks of Bellwether Media, Inc.

Editor: Betsy Rathburn      Designer: Jeffrey Kollock

Printed in the United States of America, North Mankato, MN.

# TABLE OF CONTENTS

# UNDER FIRE

The troops are under attack! Bullets rain down.
None hit the troops. But they must fire back to
save themselves.

They ready a rocket to launch at an armored vehicle. The rocket travels fast and far. In a flash, it knocks out the vehicle's gun. The troops stay safe!

# WHAT IS ADVANCED WEAPONRY?

Advanced weaponry is the use of the latest science and technology to make weapons. Weapons may be guns or **missiles**. They may also be large armored vehicles such as **tanks**.

Advanced weapons may be remote-controlled, too. This includes **unmanned aerial vehicles** (UAVs) and **unmanned ground vehicles** (UGVs). Advanced weapons help troops complete their work. They make jobs quicker and safer!

# TIMELINE

**1884**

FIRST FULLY AUTOMATIC WEAPON

**1915**

FIRST TANKS

**1945**

FIRST NUCLEAR BOMB ATTACK

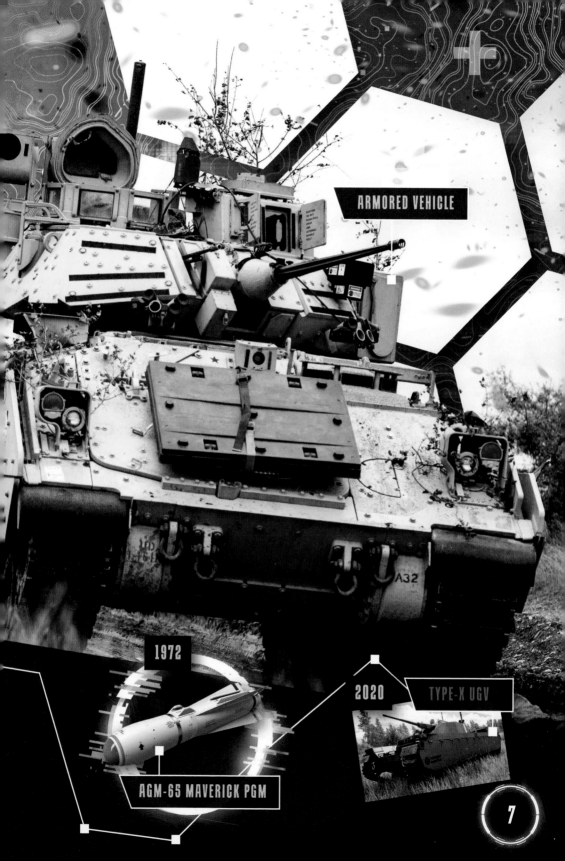

ARMORED VEHICLE

1972

AGM-65 MAVERICK PGM

2020

TYPE-X UGV

There are many types of advanced weapons. Guns are important for soldiers. Most can fire many bullets in only one second! Some fire lasers. Some can stop air attacks!

**Precision-guided munitions** (PGMs) are bombs or missiles with great aim. They can come within 10 feet (3 meters) of their marks.

**BETTER BOMB**

PGMs are much better than unguided bombs. Unguided bombs hit their targets only about 5 out of every 100 times!

PGMs

The military uses advanced vehicles, too. The Boeing Laser Avenger holds a powerful laser. This weapon can take down UAVs.

BOEING LASER AVENGER

THERMAL IMAGING

# ADVANCED WEAPONRY PROFILE

## TYPE-X UGV

**RELEASED:** 2020

**FEATURES:** LIGHTWEIGHT UGV THAT CARRIES POWERFUL WEAPONS AND CAN BE CONTROLLED FROM FAR AWAY

Some vehicles have tools to spot enemies. **Thermal imaging** picks up heat that people and vehicles give off. Laser **range finders** show how far away enemies are. They also help guide shots!

Some weapons are remote-controlled.
UAVs do not have a pilot. Pilots are
far away. They tell UAVs where to fly.
They give the command to strike!

MQ-9 REAPER UAV

The military is testing robot weapons, too. They carry guns into dangerous places. Troops tell the robots when to fire!

W-MUTT ROBOT

ROBO SOLDIER

MAARS is a military robot. It is armed with a gun and a grenade launcher!

# THE SCIENCE BEHIND ADVANCED WEAPONRY

AGM-65 MAVERICK PGM

All military weapons use different technology. PGMs are **programmed** with a flight path. An aircraft flies over a target and drops the PGM.

# HOW PGMs WORK

**2**
GPS SATELLITES SEND THE PGM INFORMATION TO PINPOINT THE TARGET'S LOCATION

**1**
AIRCRAFT DROPS PGM NEAR TARGET

**3**
PGM HITS TARGET

ANG AFRC
TEST CENTER

**GPS satellites** send the PGM information about the target's location. The PGM uses the information to hit the target!

**Radio waves** are often used for remote-controlled weapons. Troops make commands on a controller. The controller sends radio waves to the weapon. The radio waves tell the weapon where to move and when to launch.

The weapon sends radio waves back.
The radio waves contain pictures of
where the weapon is located!

# THE FUTURE OF ADVANCED WEAPONRY

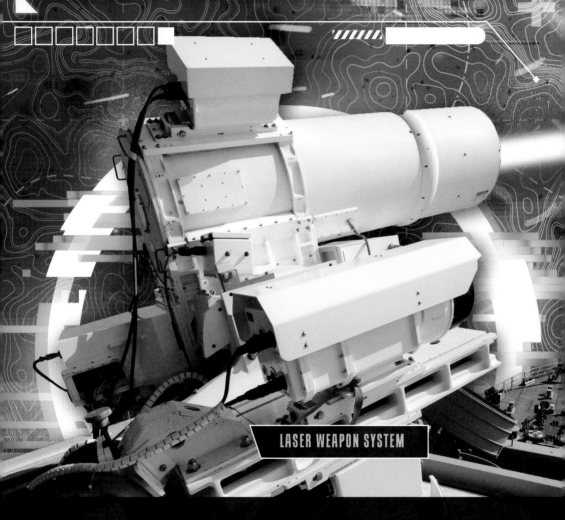

LASER WEAPON SYSTEM

Future advanced weapons will be even more powerful. Militaries are making better laser weapons. These weapons shoot faster than others. They have unlimited **ammo**!

# FUTURE
# ADVANCED WEAPONRY
# PROFILE

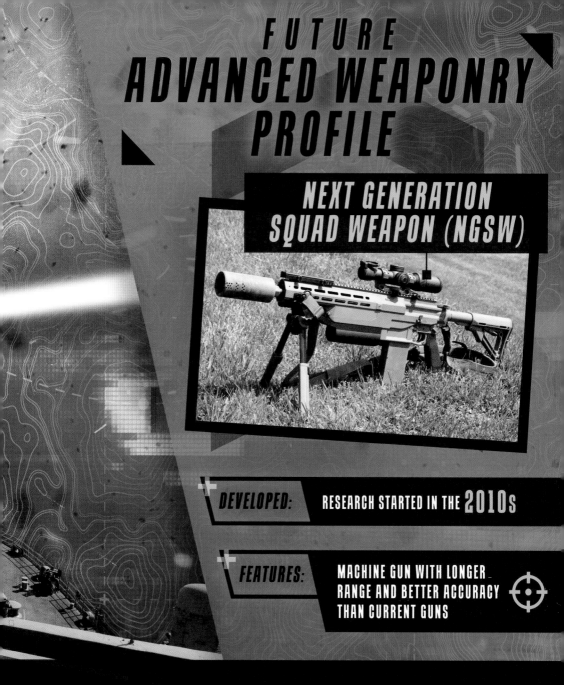

## NEXT GENERATION SQUAD WEAPON (NGSW)

**DEVELOPED:** RESEARCH STARTED IN THE **2010s**

**FEATURES:** MACHINE GUN WITH LONGER RANGE AND BETTER ACCURACY THAN CURRENT GUNS

**Hypersonic weapons** will be able to reach targets much faster. They travel over 4,000 miles (6,437 kilometers) per hour!

Militaries are making new bomber planes, too. The B-21 Raider is a future bomber. It will be able to drop powerful weapons!

# N-MILITARY USES

### AGES

VES

### POLICE RAIDS

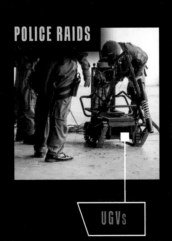

UGVs

### MEDICAL TREATMENT

LASERS

FUTURE ARMORED VEHICLE

B-21 RAIDER

Advanced weapons help troops do their jobs.
They are faster and safer than older weapons.
Future weapons hold even more possibilities!

# GLOSSARY

**ammo**—things such as bullets that are shot from guns and other weapons

**GPS satellites**—spacecraft that use GPS to determine locations on Earth; GPS stands for global positioning system.

**hypersonic weapons**—weapons that can travel more than five times faster than the speed of sound

**missiles**—powerful weapons that carry explosives

**precision-guided munitions**—weapons that use GPS, lasers, and other technology to closely hit targets; they are often called PGMs.

**programmed**—provided with instructions to do a certain thing

**radio waves**—energy waves that are used for long-distance communication

**range finders**—instruments used with weapons to help determine the distance of a target

**tanks**—armored vehicles that carry weapons

**thermal imaging**—the method of using heat given off by people or objects to help find their locations

**unmanned aerial vehicles**—vehicles in the air that are controlled by people who are not on board; they are often called UAVs.

**unmanned ground vehicles**—vehicles on the ground that are controlled by people who are not on board; they are often called UGVs.

## AT THE LIBRARY

Chandler, Matt. *Drones*. Minneapolis, Minn.: Bellwether Media, 2022.

Doeden, Matt. *Cutting-edge Military Tech*. Minneapolis, Minn.: Lerner Publications, 2020.

Rathburn, Betsy. *Robotics*. Minneapolis, Minn.: Bellwether Media, 2022.

## ON THE WEB

# FACTSURFER

Factsurfer.com gives you a safe, fun way to find more information.

1. Go to www.factsurfer.com

2. Enter "advanced weaponry" into the search box and click 🔍.

3. Select your book cover to see a list of related content.

# INDEX

The images in this book are reproduced through the courtesy of: PX Media, front cover; OlegDoroshin, p. 3; Austin Anyzeski/ US Department of Defense, pp. 4-5; Lance Cpl. William Chockey/ US Department of Defense, p. 5; Zorro2212/ Wikimedia Commons, p. 6 (1884); Andrew Skudder/ Wikimedia Commons, p. 6 (1915); Francesco Milanese, p. 6 (1945); 1_2_3D illustration, p. 7 (1972); Milremrobotics/ Wikimedia Commons, pp. 7 (2020), 11; Army Spc. Joshua Cowden/ US Department of Defense, pp. 6-7; DVIDS, pp. 8-9 (left), 12-13, 13, 16-17, 17, 19; Stocktrek Images, Inc./ Alamy, pp. 8-9 (right), 14-15; J. Helgason, p. 9 (fun fact); Boeing Photo/ Boeing Media Room, pp. 10-11; Creative Fabric Studios, p. 10 (inset); PJF Military Collection/ Alamy, p. 13 (fun fact); John Williams/ DVIDS, pp. 18-19; Dejan Lazarevic, p. 20 (radio waves); sandyman, p. 20 (UGVs); MichaelVaulin, p. 20 (lasers); Alan Radecki/ Wikimedia Commons, pp. 20-21; Luke Allen/ DVIDS, p. 21 (inset); United States Army/ Wikimedia Commons, p. 23.